AF228622

ORLANDO MAGIC

BY ANTHONY K. HEWSON

SportsZone

An Imprint of Abdo Publishing
abdobooks.com

abdobooks.com

Published by Abdo Publishing, a division of ABDO, PO Box 398166, Minneapolis, Minnesota 55439. Copyright © 2023 by Abdo Consulting Group, Inc. International copyrights reserved in all countries. No part of this book may be reproduced in any form without written permission from the publisher. SportsZone™ is a trademark and logo of Abdo Publishing.

Printed in China.
052022
092022

Cover Photo: Michael Reaves/Getty Images Sport/Getty Images
Interior Photos: Melinda Nagy/Shutterstock Images, 1; Doug Benc/Getty Images Sport/ Getty Images, 4; Elsa/Getty Images Sport/Getty Images, 6, 9; Scott Audette/Getty Images Sport/Getty Images, 8; Al Messerschmidt/AP Images, 10, 30, 33; Stephen Dunn/Allsport/ Getty Images, 13; Tony Ranze/AFP/Getty Images, 15, 17, 26; Peter Cosgrove/AP Images, 19; Jason E. Miczek/AP Images, 21; Focus on Sport/Getty Images Sport/Getty Images, 22; Bill Kostroun/AP Images, 24; Tony Ranze/AP Images, 27; Brian Cleary/AP Images, 34; Allsport/Hulton Archive/Getty Images, 36; Eric Gay/AP Images, 38; Matt Slocum/AP Images, 41

Editor: Charlie Beattie
Series Designer: Joshua Olson

Library of Congress Control Number: 2021951666

Publisher's Cataloging-in-Publication Data

Names: Hewson, Anthony K., author.
Title: Orlando Magic / by Anthony K. Hewson
Description: Minneapolis, Minnesota : Abdo Publishing, 2023 | Series: Inside the NBA |
    Includes online resources and index.
Identifiers: ISBN 9781532198397 (lib. bdg.) | ISBN 9781098272043 (ebook)
Subjects: LCSH: Orlando Magic (Basketball team)--Juvenile literature. | Basketball-
    -Juvenile literature. | Professional sports--Juvenile literature. | Sports
    franchises--Juvenile literature.
Classification: DDC 796.32364--dc23

TABLE OF CONTENTS

CHAPTER ONE

SUPERMAN SOARS

Dwight Howard had a nearly superhuman task in Game 6 of the 2009 Eastern Conference finals. One win was all his Orlando Magic needed to reach the championship series. But standing in their way were LeBron James and the visiting Cleveland Cavaliers. James was one of the best players in the National Basketball Association (NBA). Many say he's one of the best players in league history.

Howard was not the Magic's only key player, but he needed to be big in Game 6. Star point guard Jameer Nelson had not played in four months due to a shoulder injury. Forward Hedo Türkoğlu had played well earlier in the series. But in Game 6 he was having an off night. If Howard could not outplay James, the Magic were in big trouble. But the big center was ready to live up to his nickname: Superman.

Dwight Howard powers home a dunk during Game 6 of the 2009 Eastern Conference finals against the Cleveland Cavaliers.

Howard, *right*, averaged 25.8 points and 13.0 rebounds in the Eastern Conference finals, while Cleveland star LeBron James poured in 38.5 points per game.

Few had expected the Magic to make such a deep playoff run. Most experts thought the conference final would feature James and the Cavs against the defending champion Boston Celtics. But the Magic knocked off those Celtics in the Eastern Conference semifinals. And now in Game 6 of the conference finals they had pushed the Cavs to the brink of elimination.

Howard wasted no time getting started. Seconds into the game, he got the ball just inside the three-point line. After sizing up his opponent, the 6-foot-10-inch Howard drove to the hoop for an easy layup. The quick 2–0 lead got the home crowd roaring.

Superman was just warming up. With the help of some thunderous dunks, he had 13 points after one quarter. But the multitalented James also scored 13 to keep Cleveland close. The Magic led 30–25.

EARNING RESPECT

Known for being at his best in the low post, Howard was scoring from everywhere in the second quarter. A combination of dunks and hook shots helped Orlando pull away. Most importantly, Howard made his free throws. He was not normally a strong foul shooter. But he made 12 of 16 in Game 6.

Teammates

LeBron James and Dwight Howard knew each other well. In the summer of 2008, the two had been teammates on the US Olympic team. They helped Team USA win a gold medal in Beijing, China. They would later team up again on the Los Angeles Lakers in 2019.

Orlando took an 18-point lead into halftime. The Magic were 24 minutes away from reaching the second NBA Finals in team history. Howard remembered a time when there weren't so many wins or fans in Orlando. When he arrived in 2004, the Magic were struggling just to be taken seriously.

"I felt that we were a laughingstock around the league," Howard said after the game. "Everybody played the Magic,

Howard goes up for two of the 40 points he scored in Game 6.

and they thought about Disney World. So I just wanted to change that."

SUPER SECOND HALF

Howard and the Magic stayed hot in the second half. Superman was dominating in the paint. He scored 10 third-quarter points. When Cleveland threw extra defenders at him, Howard passed to open teammates. Three of his four assists came in the third quarter. The Cavaliers had no answers. For his final points of the third quarter, Howard went up and grabbed Türkoğlu's missed shot. Then Howard slammed it back home and pointed up to the crowd. The Magic were up by 16, and the celebration was on.

The Orlando fans barely sat down during the fourth quarter. Howard led all scorers with nine points in the final twelve minutes. That gave him 40 for the game. He also pitched in 14 rebounds.

As time expired, Howard tossed up a three-pointer. He missed, but it was just for fun. Orlando had already locked up the win. Superman was all smiles as he absorbed the cheers from the crowd.

Superman had won the showdown. Winning the next series for an NBA championship would be an even greater feat. But the Magic's superhero was going to give it his all.

Howard salutes the Orlando crowd after the Magic knocked off Cleveland to reach the 2009 NBA Finals.

CHAPTER TWO

O-TOWN BASKETBALL

The NBA was looking to expand in the 1980s. But the league wasn't looking at central Florida. It took Orlando native Jimmy Hewitt to change that. He had become a successful businessman by starting a company that managed day care centers. Bringing a pro sports team to his hometown was his next big idea.

The thought came to him in the mid-1980s. Hewitt had become friends with Philadelphia 76ers general manager Pat Williams. In 1985 Williams asked Hewitt which Florida city would be best for an NBA team: "Miami, Tampa, or Jacksonville?"

"Orlando is the place to be," Hewitt replied.

Hewitt was probably the only person who felt that way. Compared to other cities with NBA teams, Orlando wasn't

Nick Anderson was one of the young players who provided some positive moments in an otherwise difficult first three seasons for Orlando.

very big. It had no other major pro sports teams. Orlando was known as the home of the Walt Disney World amusement park and not much else. However, Hewitt believed in his city. He knew that Orlando was a better fit for an NBA team than anyone realized.

Hewitt pitched his idea, hoping Williams could bring some NBA knowledge to the project. There would be a lot of challenges to overcome, including building Orlando an NBA arena. In April 1986, Hewitt told Williams that he was the final piece of the puzzle. The owner wouldn't go forward without Williams as his general manager.

Williams, looking for a new challenge, was in. The two men appeared at a press conference in June announcing their intent to bring an NBA team to central Florida. They took their first $100 deposit toward season tickets that day.

The team had its founder, its general manager, and its first ticket buyers. Its home court would soon be built. All it needed next was a name.

Rejected Names

The other nickname finalists besides Magic were Heat, Tropics, and Juice. "Heat" was rejected because the ownership group thought it seemed too negative. However, a new team in Miami would adopt that name several months later. "Juice" was also a contender, but a cold winter in 1987 had just done major damage to Orlando's citrus fields.

The owners held a naming contest in an Orlando newspaper. Fans submitted more than 4,000 ideas. One of the finalists was "Magic," in reference to the city's association with Disney World. While deciding, Williams's seven-year-old daughter Karyn came to visit him from their home in Philadelphia.

Guard Dennis Scott dribbles against the Los Angeles Lakers in 1990.

"I really like this place," Karyn told her dad. "This place is like magic."

The owners were leaning toward "Magic" already. Karyn's comment put them over the edge. The team was officially named the Orlando Magic on July 27, 1986.

MAKING MAGIC

The team still was not officially part of the NBA. The Orlando owners had put everything in place for the league to say yes. On April 22, 1987, the NBA announced Orlando was in, starting in the 1989–90 season.

The first time fans got to see their new team in action came in an exhibition game before the start of the regular season. Since they don't count, exhibition games are usually not very noisy. But Orlando fans were excited. A crowd of 15,000 roared all game long. The Magic made the night memorable for the home fans. They beat the reigning NBA champion Detroit Pistons 118–109.

The regular season did not go as well. Expansion teams usually struggle to win games. The Magic were no different. Their roster was full of players other teams did not want, as well as young, inexperienced players. After starting 7–7, the Magic went just 11–57 the rest of the way. They finished last in their division.

The Magic suffered a lot of losses in their first three seasons. In 1991–92 they finished dead last in the Eastern Conference at 21–61. The bright side of that losing season was getting a chance at the top draft pick. And in 1992, there was no doubt who that pick would be. Everyone wanted the player known simply as Shaq.

THE SHAQ ERA

Shaquille O'Neal was a 7-foot-1-inch center out of Louisiana State University. With his unmatched power, he could change a game all by himself. Things were looking up for the Magic when they won the draft lottery.

Drafting Shaquille O'Neal in 1992 gave Orlando its first superstar.

Adding O'Neal boosted the team immediately. The Magic improved by 20 wins in 1992–93. O'Neal was Rookie of the Year. Even so, the Magic just barely missed the playoffs.

That ended up being a good thing. Only teams that miss the playoffs are entered in the lottery for the top draft pick. In 1993 Orlando was not likely to win the lottery. But it got lucky and won the top pick again. The team used it to select power forward Chris Webber from the University of Michigan. Minutes later the Magic traded him for the third pick, point guard Anfernee "Penny" Hardaway, as well as three future first-round picks.

Hardaway proved to be the perfect partner for O'Neal. The pair combined with shooting guard Nick Anderson to take Orlando on a thrilling run to the 1994 playoffs. They were swept in their opening series by the Indiana Pacers. Still, Orlando fans could feel something building.

The Magic made a key addition to improve their playoff hopes before the 1994–95 season. Forward Horace Grant had been a big part of three Chicago Bulls' championships. After signing in Orlando, he gave the Magic another inside scoring option alongside O'Neal.

The move put the Magic over the top. Orlando posted the best record in the East at 57–25. The Magic won their first playoff series over the Boston Celtics. Then they knocked off Michael Jordan and the Bulls in a thrilling six-game

Guard Penny Hardaway makes a slick pass against the New Jersey Nets in 1994.

series. Finally, they got revenge on the Pacers in the Eastern Conference finals.

Orlando's storybook run ended there. The Magic were swept by the defending champion Houston Rockets. Despite

Before the NBA

The only other major professional sports team to call Orlando home were the Orlando Renegades. They played in the United States Football League for one season in 1985. But the city has a long history with pro baseball. The Washington Senators (later the Minnesota Twins) used it as their spring training home from 1936 to 1990. Many minor league baseball teams have also called Orlando home over the years.

how the season ended, the 1994–95 Magic remained a beloved team in Orlando for decades.

Magic fans prepared for another title run the next year. Their team was even better, winning 60 games. But they were no longer the best team in the East. That proved to be the Bulls, who set an NBA record with 72 wins. This time the Magic couldn't beat Jordan and company. Chicago swept the Magic out of the Eastern Conference finals in four games.

An even bigger loss followed the season. O'Neal had become one of the NBA's best players. He felt he deserved more money on a new contract. But his salary demands were too much for Orlando. So O'Neal signed with the Los Angeles Lakers in the summer of 1996.

FROM SHAQ TO T-MAC

Hardaway kept Orlando competitive. But the Magic never won another playoff series during his time with the team. By 1999 it was time to move on, and Hardaway was traded to the Phoenix Suns.

Even with all their stars gone, a gritty Magic team managed to give fans a memorable season in 1999–2000. The team had a new head coach, Doc Rivers, and a group of hardworking players. No one in the NBA expected Orlando to be competitive. But they just missed the playoffs, finishing 41–41. Rivers loved the team. He called them the "Heart and Hustle" Magic.

Magic guard Darrell Armstrong, *left,* tries to dribble around David Wesley of the Charlotte Hornets during a 1999 game.

With plenty of money to spend on new players, the Magic signed Tracy McGrady in 2000. The young guard was one of the league's most promising stars. Orlando also signed All-Star forward Grant Hill.

McGrady developed into an All-Star. But Hill struggled with injuries. He played just 47 games in his first four years with the Magic. McGrady led the NBA in scoring twice, but it wasn't enough to even win a playoff series. In 2004 McGrady was traded to the Rockets.

THE HOWARD ERA

The Magic had settled into a familiar pattern. One superstar exits and another one enters. In 2004 it was Dwight Howard. He came to the NBA straight from high school. The Magic believed the towering center could be a special player and drafted him first overall. Howard rewarded that decision by averaging a double-double in his rookie season.

The Magic patiently built around Howard. He was their star on both offense and defense. In 2008 Orlando won its first postseason series since 1995. The next year, Howard was named NBA Defensive Player of the Year. The Magic beat LeBron James and the Cleveland Cavaliers to return to the NBA Finals. Just like in 1995, Orlando lost in the Finals. The Los Angeles Lakers claimed the title in a five-game series.

Unfortunately 2009 was as close as the Magic would get to a championship. They lost in the conference finals the next year. Howard was worried the Magic weren't doing enough to win it all. He requested a trade after the 2010–11 season.

Howard eventually got his wish. He was traded to the Lakers in August 2012. One of the players the Magic got back was Nikola Vučević. The 6-foot-10-inch center spent the previous season coming off the bench for the Philadelphia 76ers. Orlando made him a starter. He was one of the Magic's most reliable players.

Nikola Vučević averaged a double-double seven times in his nine seasons with the Magic.

The Magic still struggled to win games. Orlando did not draft well, and the team was unable to build a winner around Vučević. The Magic had losing records from 2012–13 to 2017–18 before reaching the playoffs each of the next two years. Both seasons ended with first-round exits. The Magic traded Vučević in March 2021 and started another rebuilding project. Fans had to be a little patient to see their next young core develop.

CHAPTER THREE

MAGIC MEN

With one swat of his hand, Nick Anderson became a Magic legend forever. In Game 1 of the 1995 Eastern Conference semifinals, Anderson pursued Michael Jordan as the Chicago Bulls' guard brought the ball up the court. There was less than a minute to play. As Jordan looked to set up a play, Anderson batted the ball away, and Penny Hardaway picked it up. He dished to Horace Grant, who slammed home a dunk to give Orlando a 92–91 lead. The Magic went on to win the game and were off and running in their series.

Anderson was more to Magic fans than just one play. He was the first draft pick in team history. And he was a steady and reliable player who ranks among the Magic's all-time leaders in many categories. But Anderson was not the kind of superstar player who could transform a team.

Nick Anderson was the Magic's first-ever draft pick. The team selected him eleventh overall in 1989.

Shaquille O'Neal (32) and Magic guard Dennis Scott (3) walk off the floor as arena staff look over the broken backboard at Meadowlands Arena on April 23, 1993.

That player for the Magic was center Shaquille O'Neal. In 1992 they won the draft lottery. Orlando had just a one-in-11 chance of winning the first pick. On draft day, more than 10,000 fans packed Orlando Arena to watch on the big screen as the team landed O'Neal.

Few players in NBA history have transformed a team like O'Neal. He was an almost-unstoppable force. At 285 pounds, he could power his way to the hoop. But O'Neal also had soft hands and a good shooting touch. He averaged 27.2 points and 12.5 rebounds per game in Orlando. He also delivered on defense as one of the league's best shot blockers.

Shaq's power was obvious even in his rookie season. While playing in Phoenix against the Suns on February 7, 1993, O'Neal dunked so hard that the backboard collapsed. Later that season, O'Neal broke another backboard during a game against the Nets in New Jersey. O'Neal was so big and strong that the NBA had to change how backboards were made.

The perfect complement to O'Neal arrived in 1993. Penny Hardaway was the do-it-all guard who could both score and set up O'Neal inside. Hardaway was also a great defender. His 1.9 steals per game are still the most in team history. His play boosted the Magic from playoff team to championship contender.

BUILDING TOWARD THE FINALS

Coaching the Magic in the mid-1990s led to Brian Hill racking up more wins than anyone else in team history. Hill started as an assistant in 1990 under Orlando's first head coach, Matt Guokas. He then took over for Guokas before the 1993–94 season. Over the next three and a half seasons, Hill had a record of 191–104. He returned to coach Orlando again for another two-year stint starting in 2005.

It was very difficult for opposing teams to stop both O'Neal and Hardaway. That job became even tougher when veteran forward Horace Grant joined Orlando before the 1994–95 season. Grant was used to playing with two superstars. He had

Magic guard Penny Hardaway glides to the rim against the Seattle SuperSonics in 1996.

supported Michael Jordan and Scottie Pippen as the Chicago Bulls won three straight championships in the early 1990s.

Darrell Armstrong took over as the starting point guard after Hardaway left in the summer of 1999. He became a leader on the "Heart and Hustle" team that nearly reached the 2000 playoffs. But for several seasons, the Magic could never quite put it all together again. Forward Grant Hill arrived in 2000. He had been an All-Star with all-around skills for the Detroit Pistons. But he struggled to stay healthy during his seven seasons in Orlando.

Tracy McGrady grew up in Central Florida idolizing Hardaway. The Magic traded for the high-flying shooting guard in 2000, hoping he could bring a spark back to the team. Over four seasons, McGrady dazzled the hometown fans with his huge dunks. "T-Mac" even led the NBA in scoring twice while wearing a Magic uniform. However, he was never able to lead Orlando out of the first round of the playoffs.

Tracy McGrady averaged a career-high 32.1 points per game during the 2002–03 season.

ANOTHER FINALS RUN

The Magic had to wait for a new star to emerge. They found one in the 2004 draft. Once again the Magic had the first pick. Emeka Okafor had been a star for the University of Connecticut. Many expected him to step in and be a good player from day one. Orlando took the riskier option. Dwight Howard came to the NBA right out of high school. But even at 18 he had all the tools to become a superstar.

Howard produced right away. He averaged a double-double in every season he played with the Magic. From 2008–09 to 2011–12, he averaged at least two blocks per game. At 6 feet, 10 inches tall and 265 pounds, Howard was a powerful inside presence. He was a fierce dunker. In 2008 he became the tallest player to ever win the dunk contest.

Howard was the centerpiece of the next Magic team to make the NBA Finals. But he didn't do it alone. Point guard Jameer Nelson was also picked in the first round of the 2004 draft by the Denver Nuggets. The Magic picked him up that same day in a trade. Nelson's playmaking ability helped Orlando back to playoff contention.

The final important piece of the 2009 Finals team was Hedo Türkoğlu. The Turkish forward played nearly 500 games for Orlando. He was an excellent ball handler and helped set up teammates for scores. It was Türkoğlu, not Howard, who led the Magic in scoring in the 2009 Finals.

The Howard era came to an end in 2012 when Orlando sent him to the Los Angeles Lakers. The trade involved multiple teams and players. One of the players Orlando got in return was Nikola Vučević. He was also a double-double machine. Vučević averaged 17.6 points and 10.8 rebounds over nine seasons with Orlando. He scored at an even better pace in his last three seasons with the Magic, averaging more than 20 points per game. But Vučević was traded in 2021 as the Magic began their search for a new superstar.

One of the players Orlando received in the Vučević trade was Wendell Carter Jr. The young center nearly averaged a double-double early in his Magic career. Point guard Cole Anthony, Orlando's top pick in 2020, showed signs he could handle the scoring load. Fans hoped these young players would be Orlando's next generation of stars.

Sixth Man

The Magic's No. 6 jersey is retired in honor of its fans. It is the only jersey the team has ever retired. Fans are sometimes referred to as the "sixth man" on a basketball team because of their support. But when the team signed NBA great Patrick Ewing in 2001, it allowed him to wear the number for his lone Magic season.

CHAPTER FOUR

MAGIC MOMENTS

Of course a team called the Magic gave its fans a show for its first regular-season game on November 4, 1989. There were laser shows, fireworks, and streams of smoke soaring through the brand-new Orlando Arena. But that was all before the game. Basketball was the main attraction.

The sold-out crowd was there to see Orlando take on the New Jersey Nets. The Magic made just 36 percent of their shots but gave New Jersey all it could handle. Orlando guard Reggie Theus poured in 21 points, and forward Terry Catledge added 25. The Magic fought hard and led the game 105–103 late in the fourth quarter. But the Nets put together an 8–1 run over the final two minutes to spoil Orlando's special night.

Fans didn't have to wait too much longer to see a win. On November 6, the Magic welcomed the New York Knicks, who had won their division the year before. Theus led the way with

Guard Reggie Theus averaged 18.9 points per game during the Magic's first season in 1989–90.

24 points. After leading at halftime, the Magic fell behind 82–79 late in the third quarter. But Orlando responded with an 11–0 run to finish the quarter.

This time, the Magic finished the job with a 118–110 victory. From there Orlando went on to a 7–7 start before ultimately finishing 18–64.

DISHING IT OUT

The early Magic teams didn't have superstars, but they had players who were hungry for opportunities. Point guard Scott Skiles was one of them. Skiles hadn't played much in his first three NBA seasons. Still, the Magic took a chance on him in the 1989 expansion draft. He emerged as a key starter in Orlando. The Magic didn't have many highlights in their early seasons either. But Skiles provided one on December 30, 1990.

With the Denver Nuggets in town, Skiles got rolling. It was like every pass he made was leading to another basket. He had racked up 14 assists by halftime. The single-game record of 29 assists had stood for 12 years. Skiles dished out 16 more helpers in the second half to break it. The Nuggets had only 14 assists as a team. Orlando won easily, 155–116.

MAGICAL RUN

As the Magic were making their run to the 1995 NBA Finals, they had to show they belonged among the NBA's best teams.

Scott Skiles spent five seasons as the Magic's starting point guard and averaged 7.2 assists per game during that time.

The Magic's Nick Anderson, *right,* chases down Michael Jordan of the Chicago Bulls. Anderson stole the ball on the play to set up an Orlando victory.

One of those was the Chicago Bulls. Superstar Michael Jordan had just returned to the NBA after a retirement lasting less than two seasons.

The Magic felt confident they could knock off the three-time champion Bulls. Maybe they were a little too confident. After winning Game 1 of their semifinal series, Magic guard Nick Anderson said, "He didn't look like the old Michael Jordan." Jordan's famous No. 23 had been retired by the Bulls, forcing him to wear a new number, 45. "Number 45 doesn't explode like Number 23 used to," Anderson also said.

In Game 2, Jordan took the court wearing 23. Anderson took a lot of criticism for his comments. But he and the Magic backed them up. Jordan played much better, but it wasn't enough. The Magic finished off the Bulls in six games.

Orlando then faced Reggie Miller and the Indiana Pacers in the conference finals. At the end of a back-and-forth series, the Magic hosted a winner-take-all Game 7. In a packed and noisy Orlando Arena, the Magic crushed Indiana 105–81. Shaquille O'Neal led the way with 25 points as the Magic made their first NBA Finals.

Anderson found himself in the spotlight again in the first game of the 1995 NBA Finals. The Magic led the Houston Rockets 110–107 with 10.5 seconds left. Orlando had the ball, and the Rockets fouled Anderson. The guard stepped up to the line with a chance to put the game away. He missed the first shot and spun away from the basket in disgust. Before his second shot he pounded his chest twice to pump himself up. His second attempt clanked off the front of the rim.

The rebound was tapped around and fell into Anderson's hands. He was fouled immediately by Houston. The normally dependable foul shooter had another chance. The stunned crowd watched on as Anderson missed again. This time his shot was long. Anderson could only smile as the fourth shot also missed.

Orlando's Shaquille O'Neal, *right,* and Hakeem Olajuwon of the Houston Rockets contest the opening tip during a 1995 NBA Finals game.

Houston grabbed the rebound. After a timeout, Rockets guard Kenny Smith tied the game on a three-pointer. The Rockets won in overtime on their way to a four-game sweep. Fans in Orlando still wonder if the 1995 Finals might have been different if Anderson had made just one shot.

MILLENNIAL MOMENTS

Few memories top what the 1994–95 Magic did as a team. But over the years, fans have been treated to some incredible individual achievements. Tracy McGrady was one of the best scorers in the NBA during his time in Orlando. But T-Mac outdid himself on March 10, 2004. He scored a team record 62 points against the Washington Wizards. McGrady joked later that he could have hit 70 had he not missed nine free throws.

Dwight Howard did not score like McGrady. Instead, he thrilled fans with his dunking and shot blocking. In 2008 Howard put himself to the test in the NBA dunk contest. He led the NBA in dunks and could definitely win. But Howard also put on a show.

Before his second dunk, Howard marked out a spot near the free throw line to jump from. He then took off his jersey to reveal a shirt with the Superman logo. Magic teammate Jameer Nelson then handed Howard a cape to complete his transformation. Howard proceeded to throw down a massive dunk and went on to win the contest.

Howard's athleticism was one big reason the Magic made a run to the 2009 NBA Finals. Teammate Hedo Türkoğlu was another spark for Orlando. Türkoğlu had a habit of producing big games when his team needed him most.

Dwight Howard skies for a dunk while dressed as Superman during the 2008 All-Star Slam Dunk Contest.

The Magic had to face the defending champion Boston Celtics in the conference semis. It was a tough series, but the Magic managed to push Boston to Game 7. In one of the biggest games in Magic history, Türkoğlu dominated with 25 points and 12 assists. He scored 10 points in the fourth quarter, including a three-pointer to put Orlando up 15 with just a few minutes left. Türkoğlu pumped his fist as he ran back down the court knowing his Magic were on their way to a win.

After Howard's performance to knock off LeBron James and the Cavaliers in the conference finals, the Magic faced the Los Angeles Lakers in the Finals. Orlando quickly fell behind 2–0 in the series. The team had lost its shooting touch. The Magic made less than 30 percent of their shots in Game 1.

The Magic turned things around in Game 3. Winning their first-ever NBA Finals game was a team effort. It was their first home Finals game since 1995. Orlando made 75 percent of its shots in the first half. That was a Finals record. The Magic shot 62.5 percent for the game, another Finals record. And they made shots in every way possible. Howard finished at the hoop. Forward Rashard Lewis made 50 percent of his three-pointers. Five players scored 18 points or more.

Unfortunately for the Magic, they could not keep up that pace. They made just 42.8 percent of their shots in the entire series. Orlando lost in five games.

Howard won his third consecutive Defensive Player of the Year award after the 2010–11 season. But a back injury for Howard signaled the beginning of the end of the Magic's title hopes. The next year, Howard needed surgery and missed a lot of time. He was traded before the start of the 2012–13 season.

Orlando received center Nikola Vučević in the Howard trade. He and teammate Tobias Harris teamed up for a historic performance in the first year of their Magic careers. On April 10, 2013, both Vučević and Harris had at least 30 points and 19 rebounds in a win over the Milwaukee Bucks. They were the first teammates to do that since 1967.

After years of struggles, Vučević led the Magic back to the playoffs in 2018–19. The team did it with a 22–9 run in its final 31 games. That hot streak carried over to Game 1 of the playoffs as the Magic upset the Toronto Raptors. But Orlando failed to win another game in the series.

Guard Jalen Suggs starred in his one season at Gonzaga University before he was selected fifth overall by the Magic in the 2021 NBA Draft.

After trading Vučević and other talented players, the Magic found themselves rebuilding again by 2021. With its first pick in the 2021 draft, Orlando selected exciting guard Jalen Suggs from Gonzaga University. Fans hoped he was the next superstar to lead the Magic to the playoffs.

TIMELINE

1986

Orlando businessman Jimmy Hewitt and NBA executive Pat Williams announce their intention to pursue an NBA expansion team for the Orlando area.

1987

The NBA officially confirms on April 22 that the Orlando Magic will begin play in the 1989–90 season.

1989

The Magic play their first game on November 4. They get their first win two days later against the New York Knicks.

1992

Orlando wins the draft lottery and uses the first overall pick to choose Shaquille O'Neal. The center wins Rookie of the Year as the Magic improve by 20 wins.

1993

The Magic win the draft lottery again. Minutes after selecting Chris Webber, they trade him for Penny Hardaway and future draft picks.

1995

The Magic make a run to the NBA Finals, where they lose in four games to the Houston Rockets.

1996

The Magic are swept in the Eastern Conference Finals by the Chicago Bulls. O'Neal leaves the Magic after the season and signs with the Los Angeles Lakers.

1999

Orlando reaches the playoffs but loses in the first round. Hardaway is traded to the Phoenix Suns in August.

2000

After losing O'Neal and Hardaway to other teams, Orlando makes a splash by signing Tracy McGrady and Grant Hill.

2004

The Magic draft high school player Dwight Howard with the first overall pick.

2009

With Howard now one of the league's top players, the Magic make it to their second NBA Finals and win a game in the Finals for the first time ever.

2012

Howard is traded to the Lakers in August in a deal that also involves the Denver Nuggets and Philadelphia 76ers. The Magic receive five draft picks and six players, including center Nikola Vučević.

2019

With new center Nikola Vučević, the Magic return to the playoffs for the first time since 2012.

FRANCHISE HISTORY
Orlando Magic (1989–)

KEY PLAYERS
Nick Anderson (1989–99)
Darrell Armstrong (1995–2003)
Horace Grant (1994–99,
 2001–02)
Anfernee Hardaway (1993–99)
Grant Hill (2000–07)
Dwight Howard (2004–12)
Tracy McGrady (2000–04)
Jameer Nelson (2004–14)
Shaquille O'Neal (1992–96)
Scott Skiles (1989–94)
Hedo Türkoğlu (2004–09,
 2010–13)
Nikola Vučević (2012–21)

KEY COACHES
Brian Hill (1993–97, 2005–07)
Stan Van Gundy (2007–12)

HOME ARENAS
Orlando Arena (1989–2010)
Amway Center (2010–)

TEAM TRIVIA

HALL OF FAMERS

In addition to Dominique Wilkins, two basketball Hall of Famers spent just a single season or less with Orlando: centers Patrick Ewing and Ben Wallace.

FIRST TO 50

The first 50-point game in Magic history didn't come from Shaquille O'Neal. It didn't come from Dwight Howard. It came from Nick Anderson. And he did it off the bench. Anderson was hurt and wasn't even sure he could play on April 23, 1993. In just 33 minutes, Anderson hit 17 of 25 shots and all 12 free throws for 50 points.

10,000 CLUB

Howard, Anderson, and Nikola Vučević are the only players who have ever scored 10,000 or more points in a Magic uniform.

SMALL-TOWN HEROES

Orlando was the smallest market in the NBA when the Magic began playing. It has since grown larger than 12 other NBA cities.

assist
A pass that leads directly to a basket.

conference
A subset of teams within a sports league.

contract
In sports, an agreement to play for a certain team.

double-double
Accumulating 10 or more of two certain statistics in a game.

expansion team
A new team that is added to an existing league.

lottery
In sports, a draw to determine the order for the upcoming draft.

paint
The colored area of the court underneath the basket.

point guard
The player who directs a team's offensive attack.

rebound
To catch the ball after a shot has been missed.

rookie
A professional athlete in his or her first year of competition.

MORE INFORMATION

BOOKS

Flynn, Brendan. *The NBA Encyclopedia for Kids.* Minneapolis, MN: Abdo Publishing, 2022.

Mahoney, Brian. *GOATs of Basketball.* Minneapolis, MN: Abdo Publishing, 2022.

Ybarra, Andres. *Great Basketball Debates.* Minneapolis, MN: Abdo Publishing, 2019.

ONLINE RESOURCES

To learn more about the Orlando Magic, please visit **abdobooklinks.com** or scan this QR code. These links are routinely monitored and updated to provide the most current information available.

ABOUT THE AUTHOR

Anthony K. Hewson is a freelance writer originally from San Diego. He and his wife now live in the San Francisco Bay Area with their two dogs.